A Walk In Winter's Garden

Adult Coloring Book
by
Armani Frederic

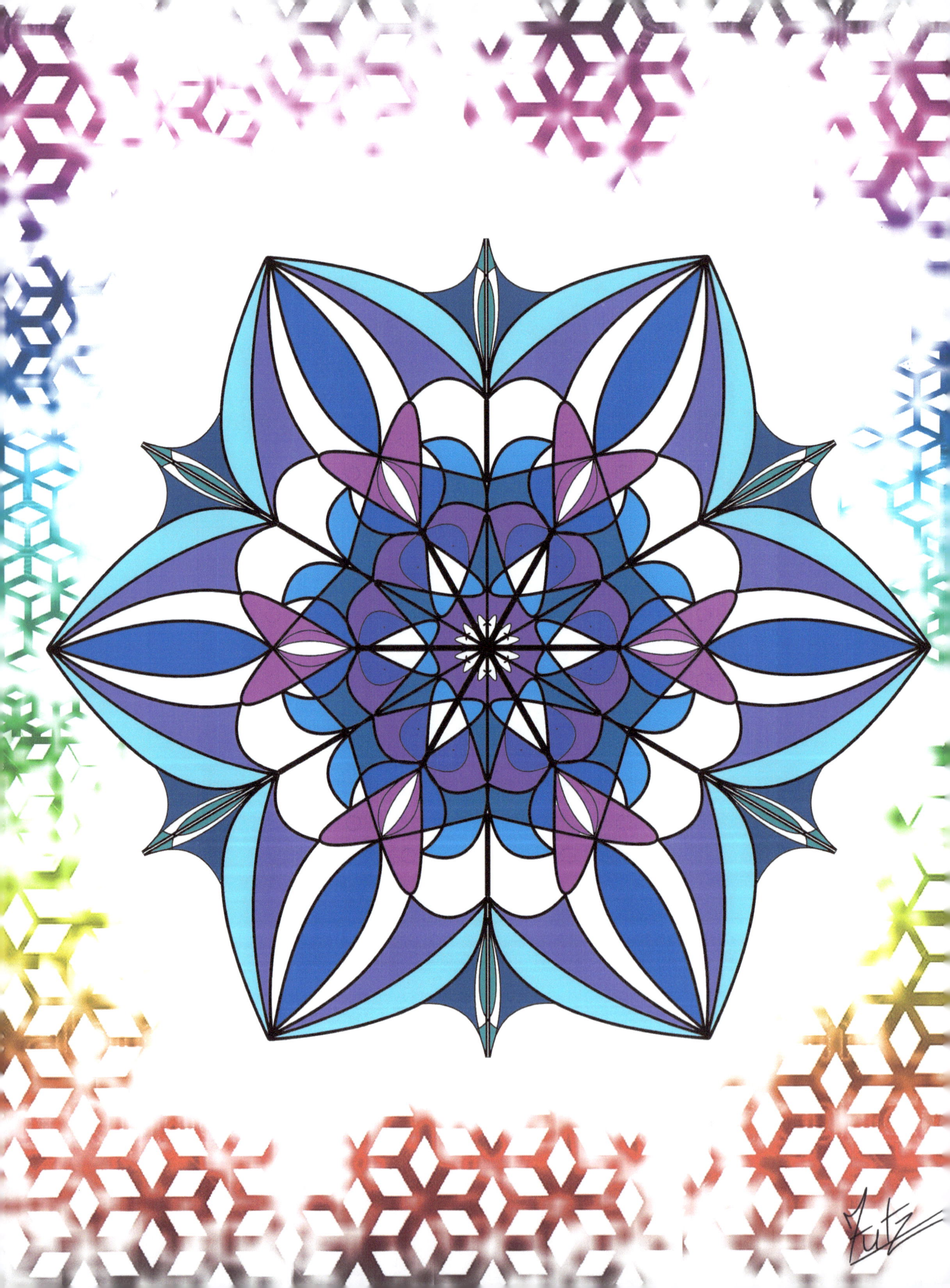

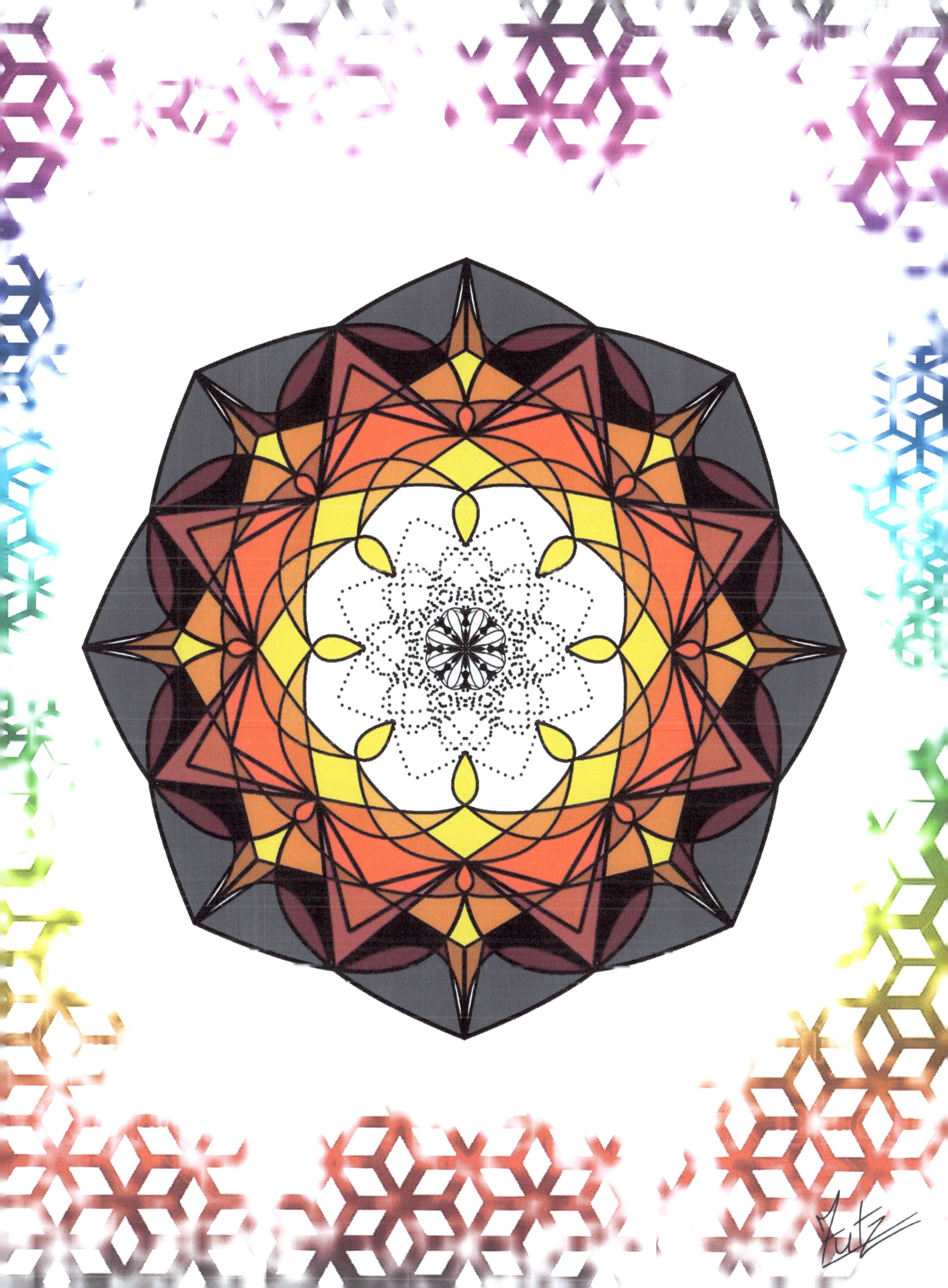

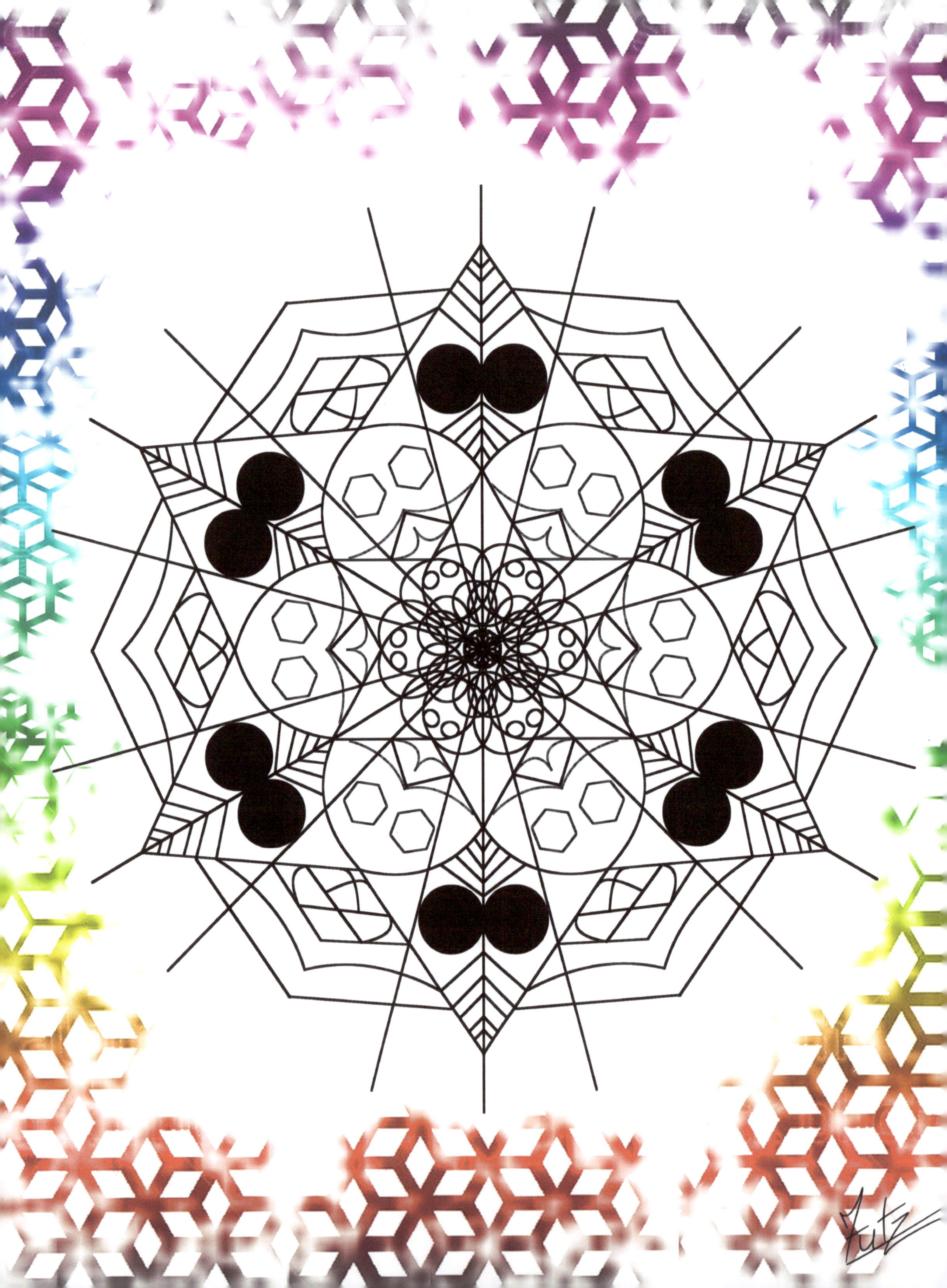

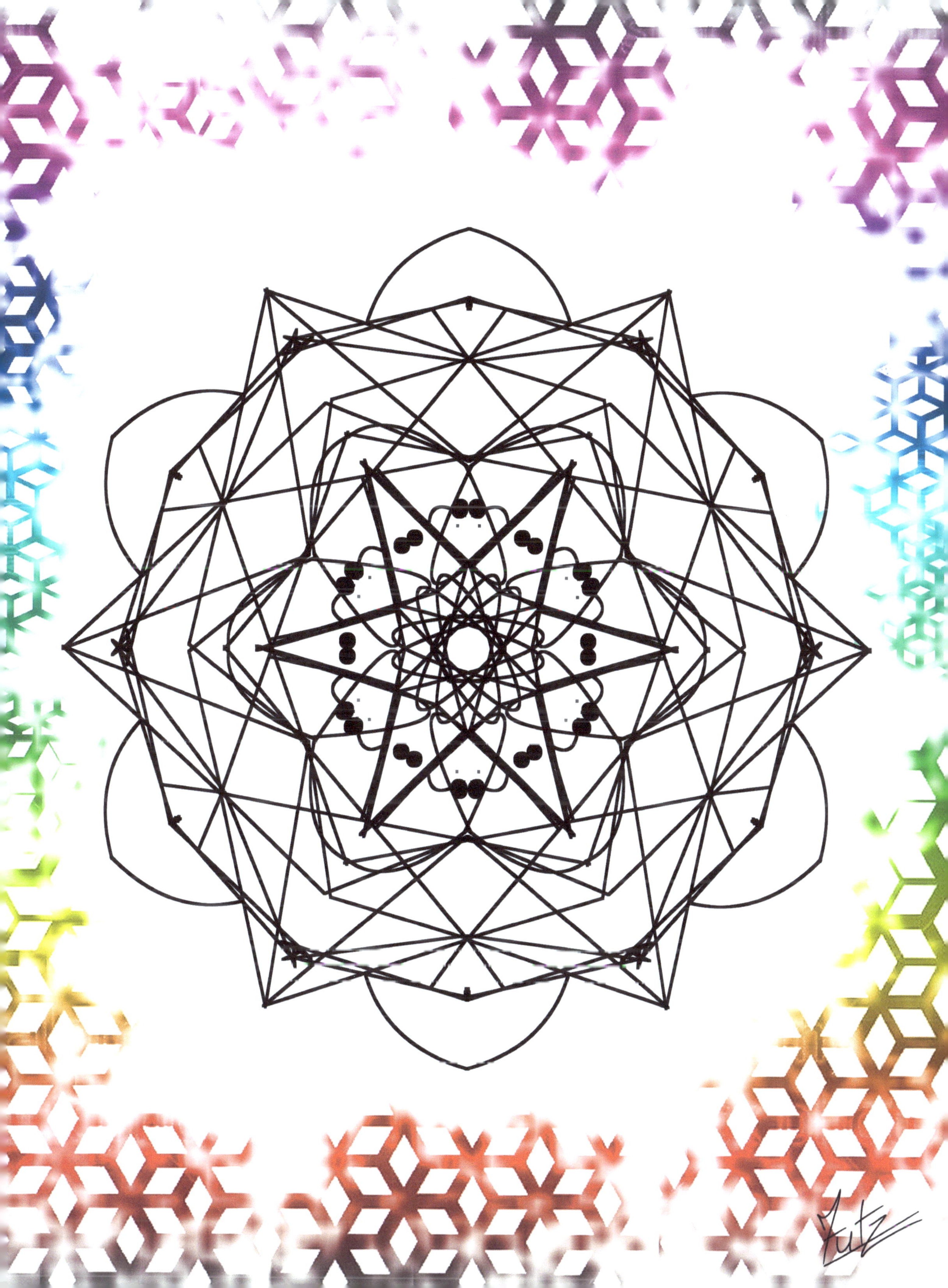

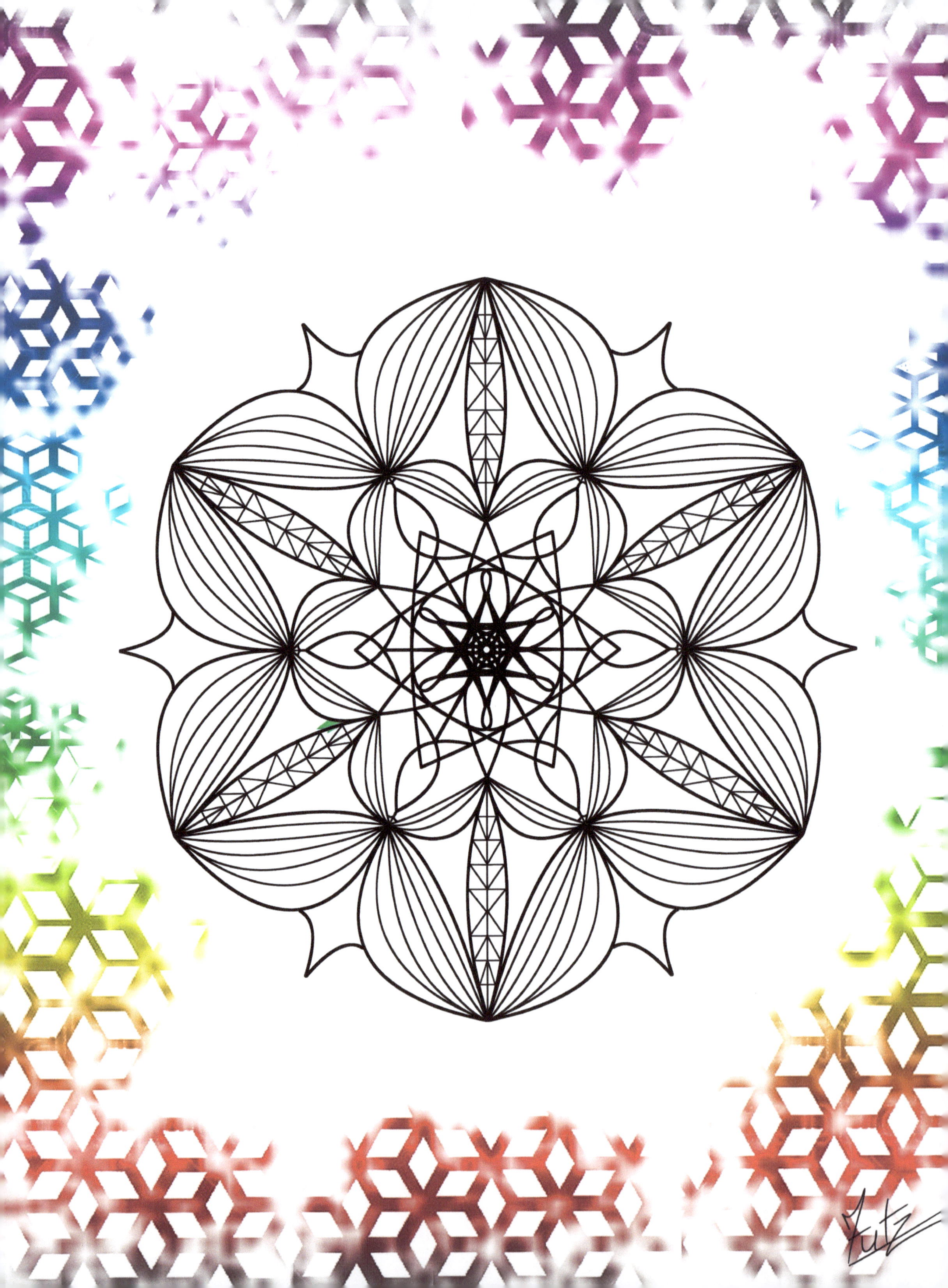

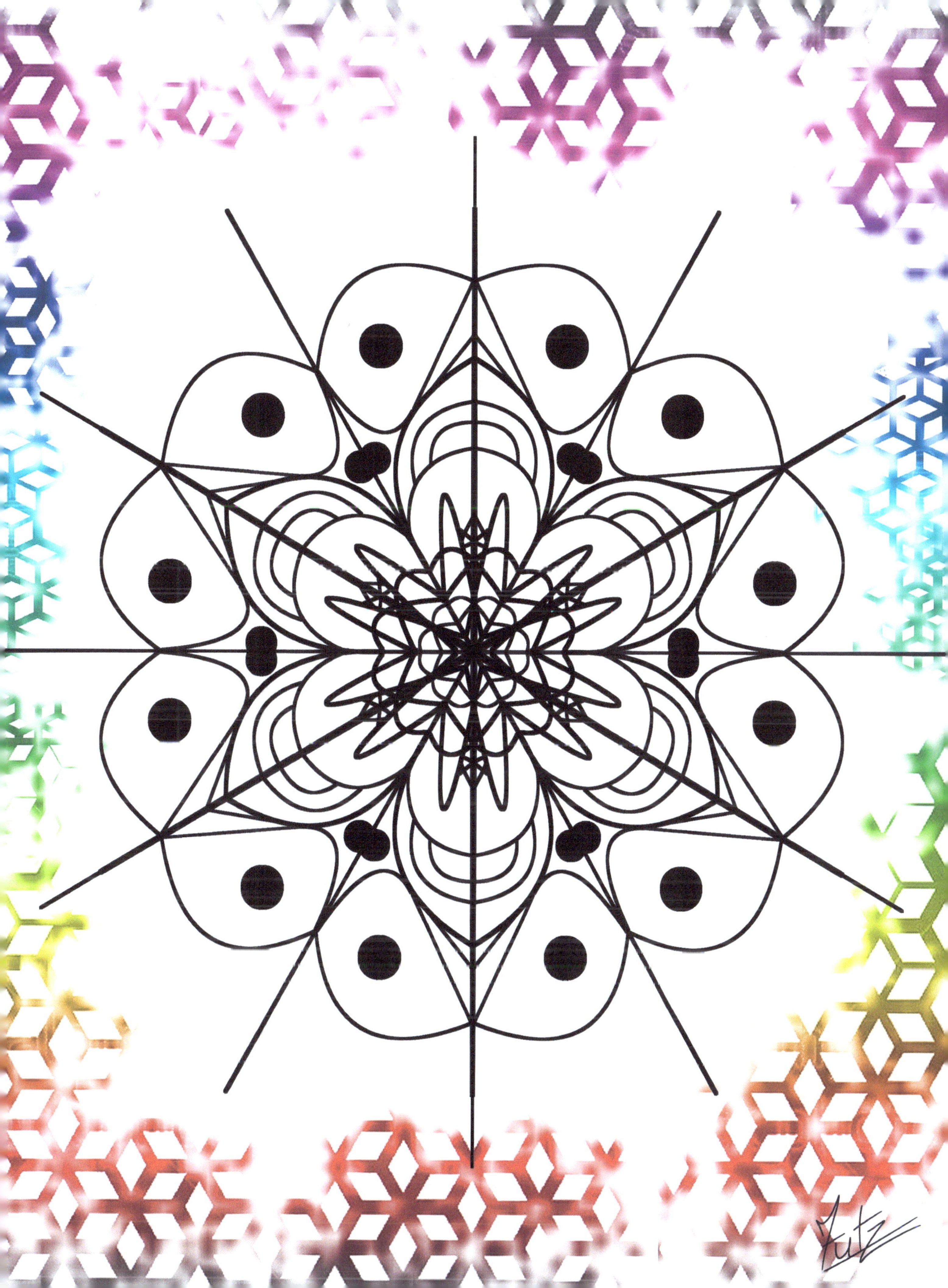

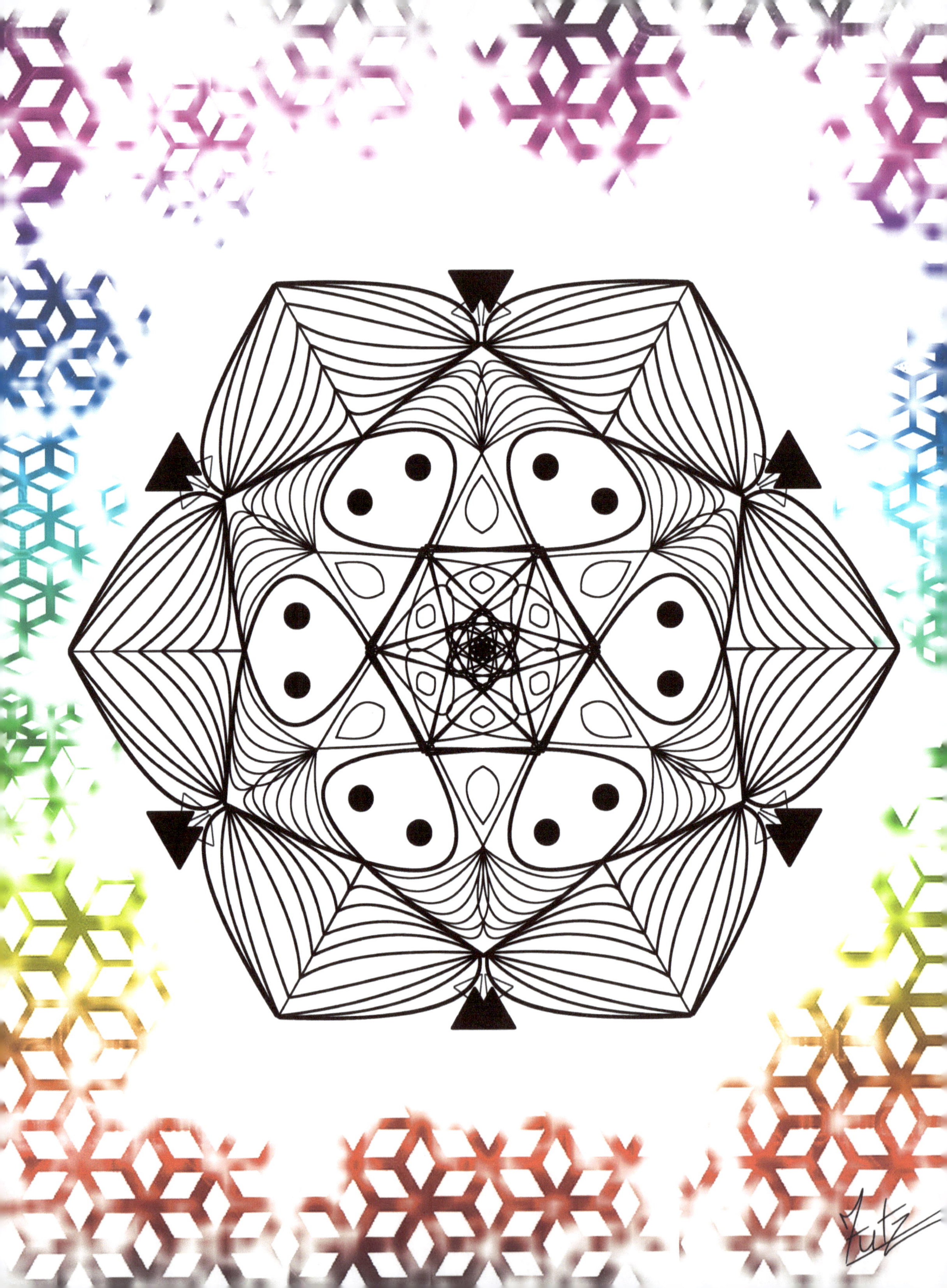

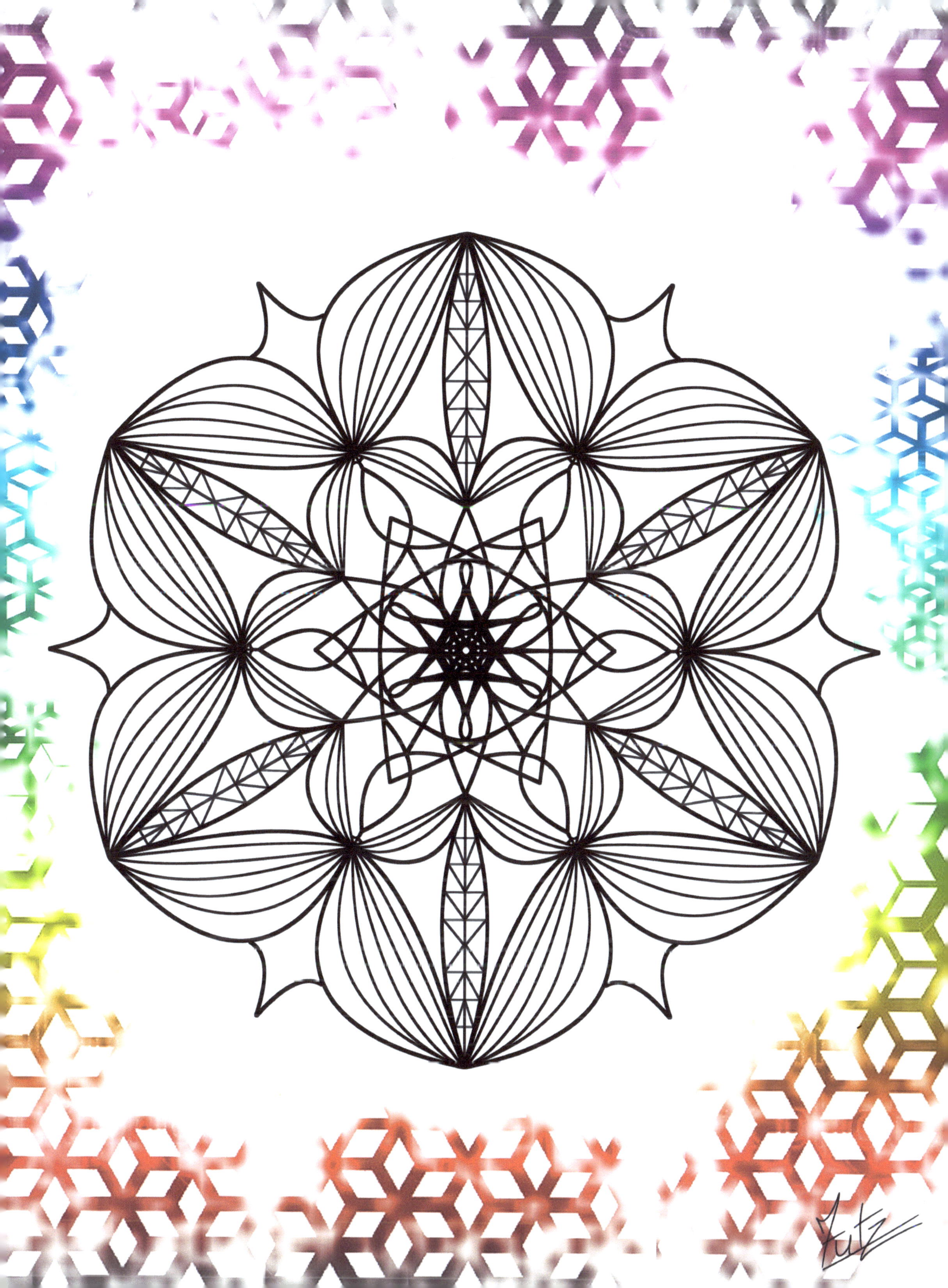

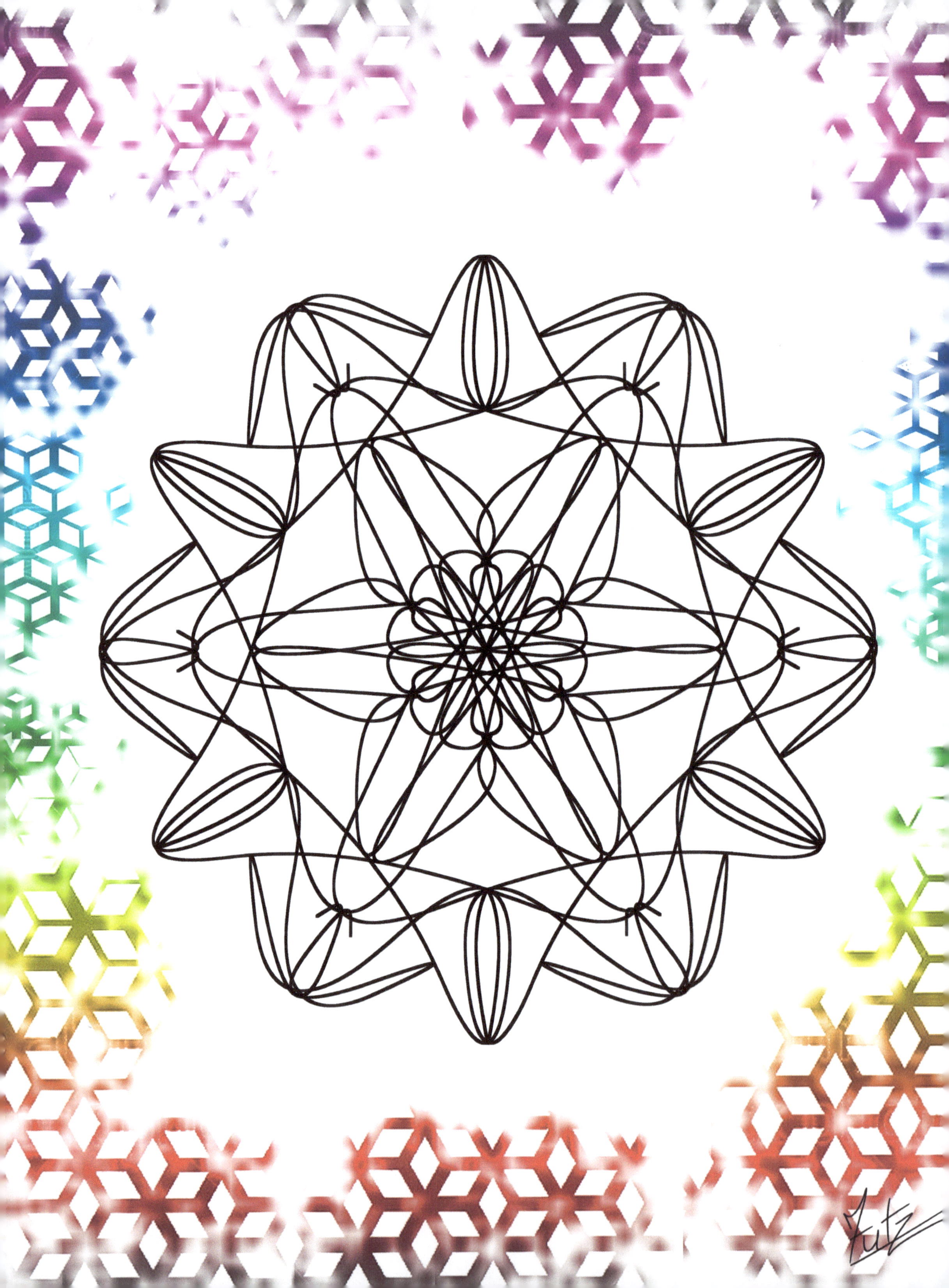

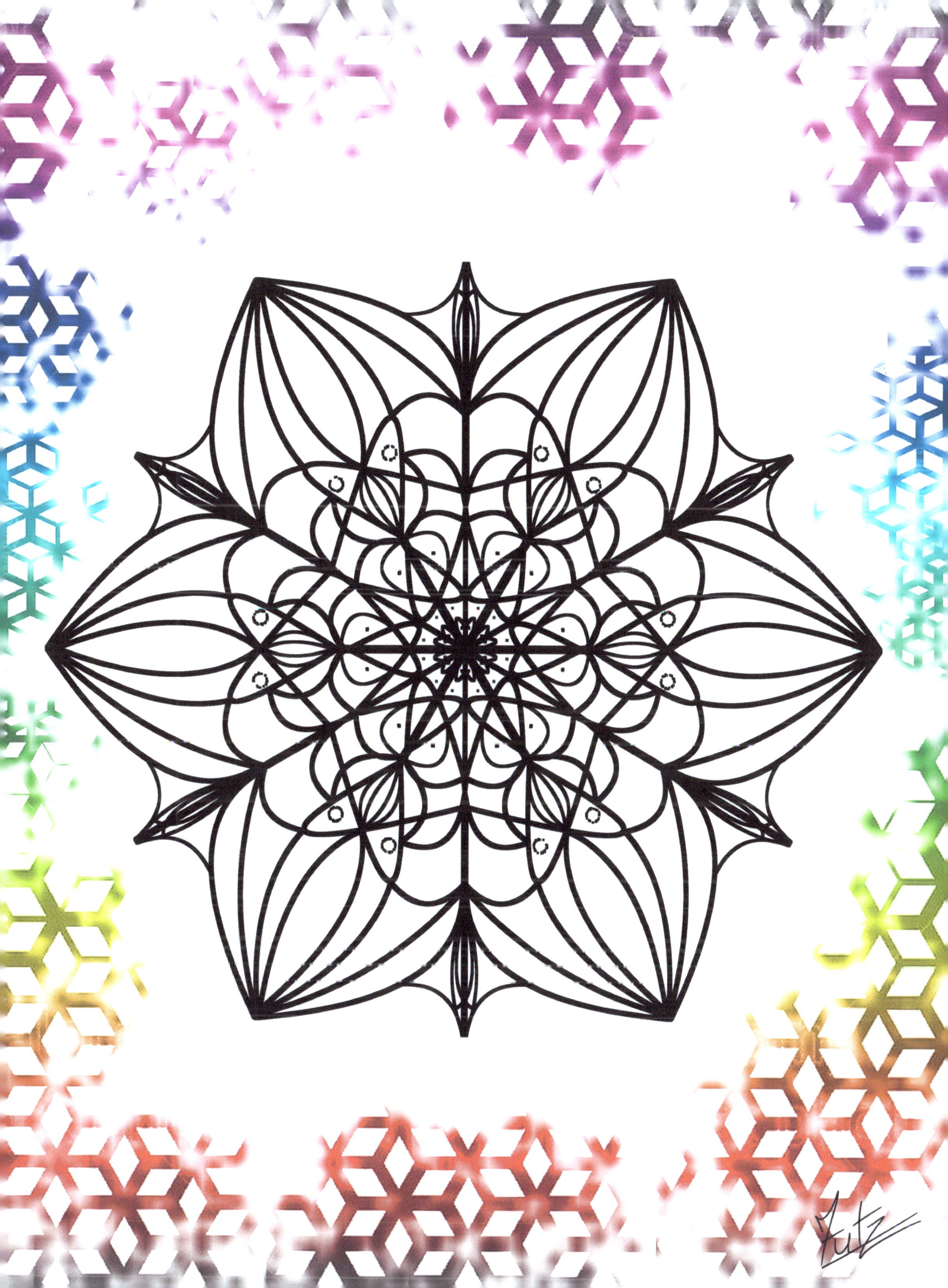

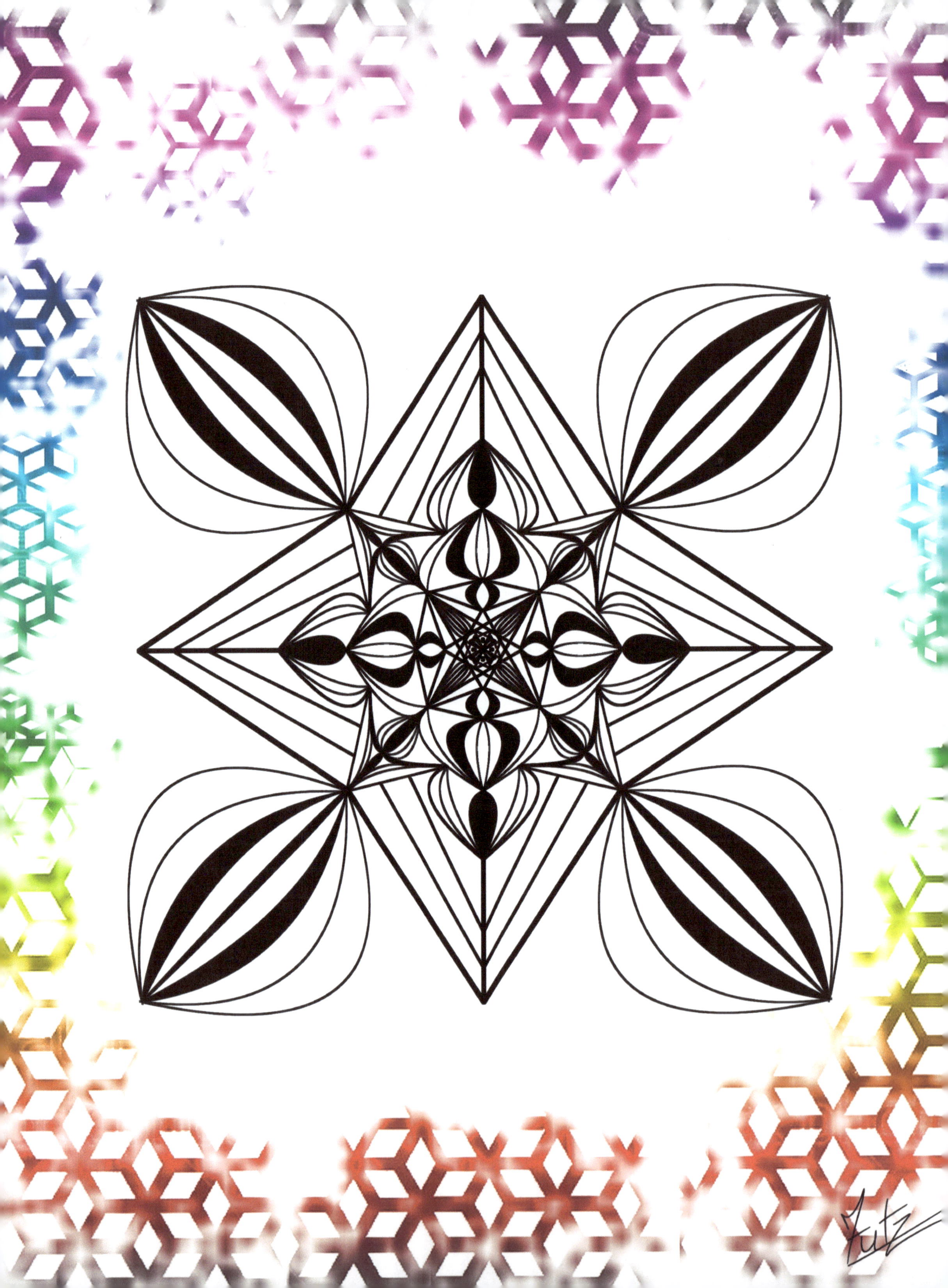

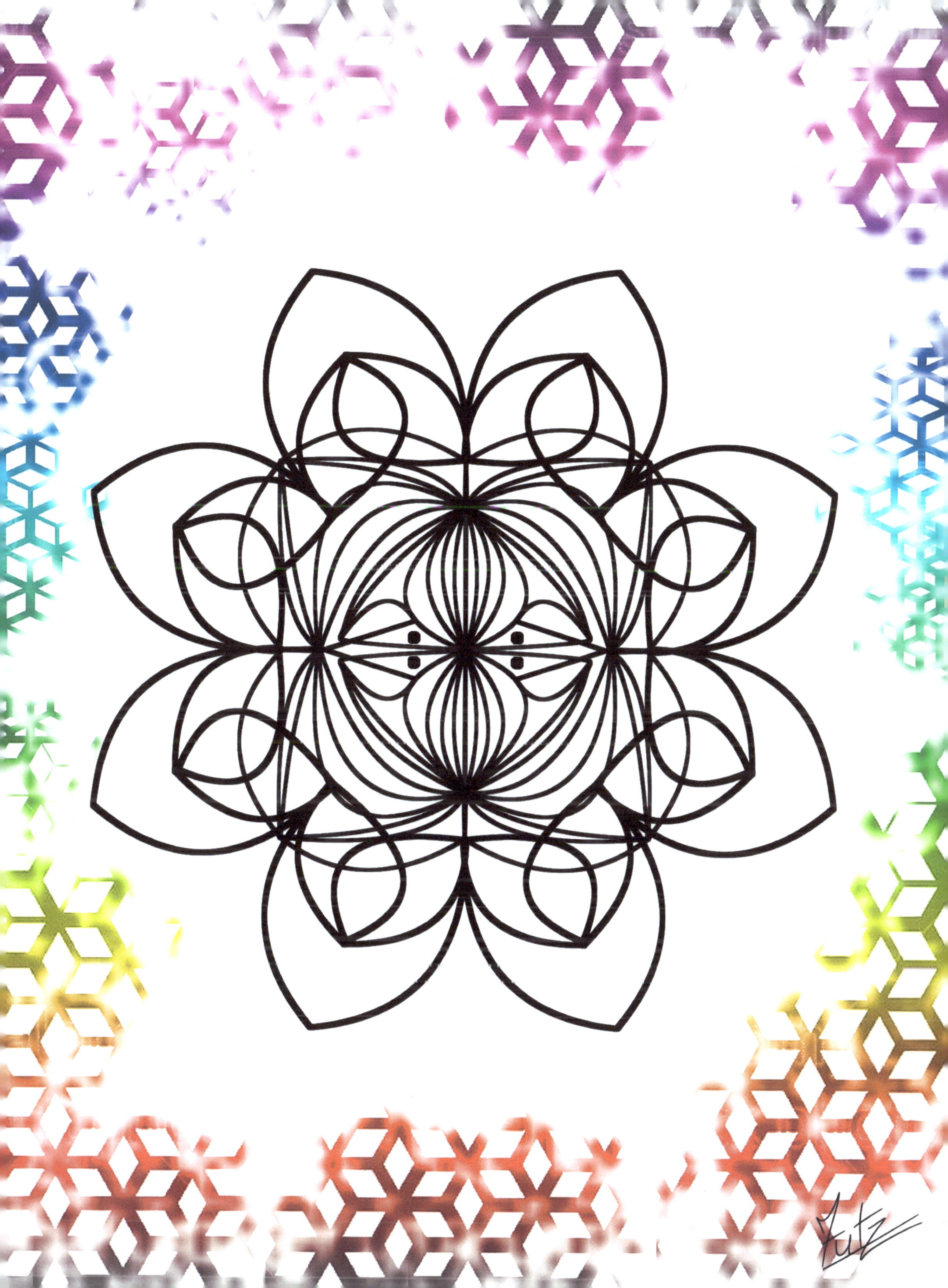
Lutz

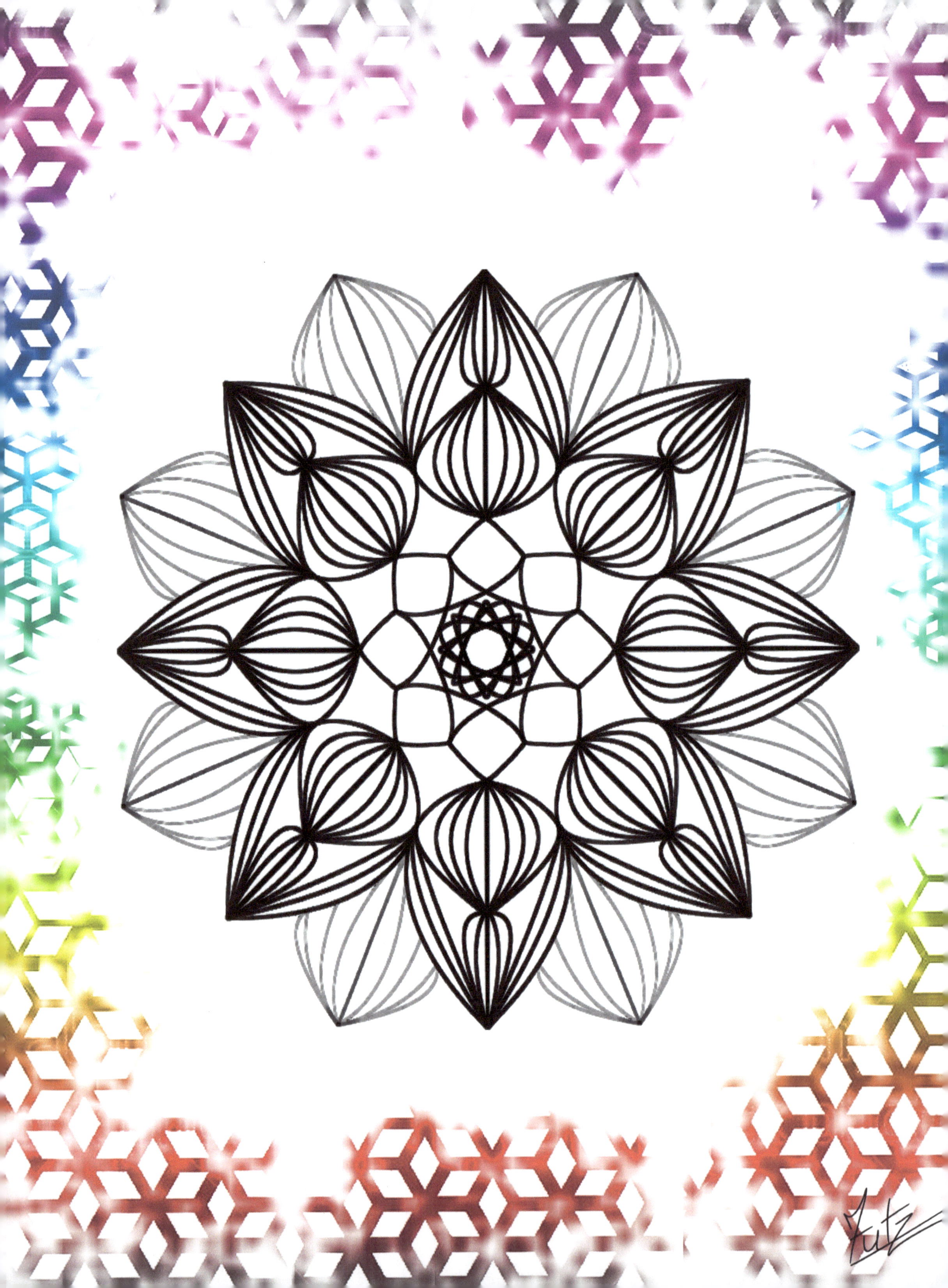

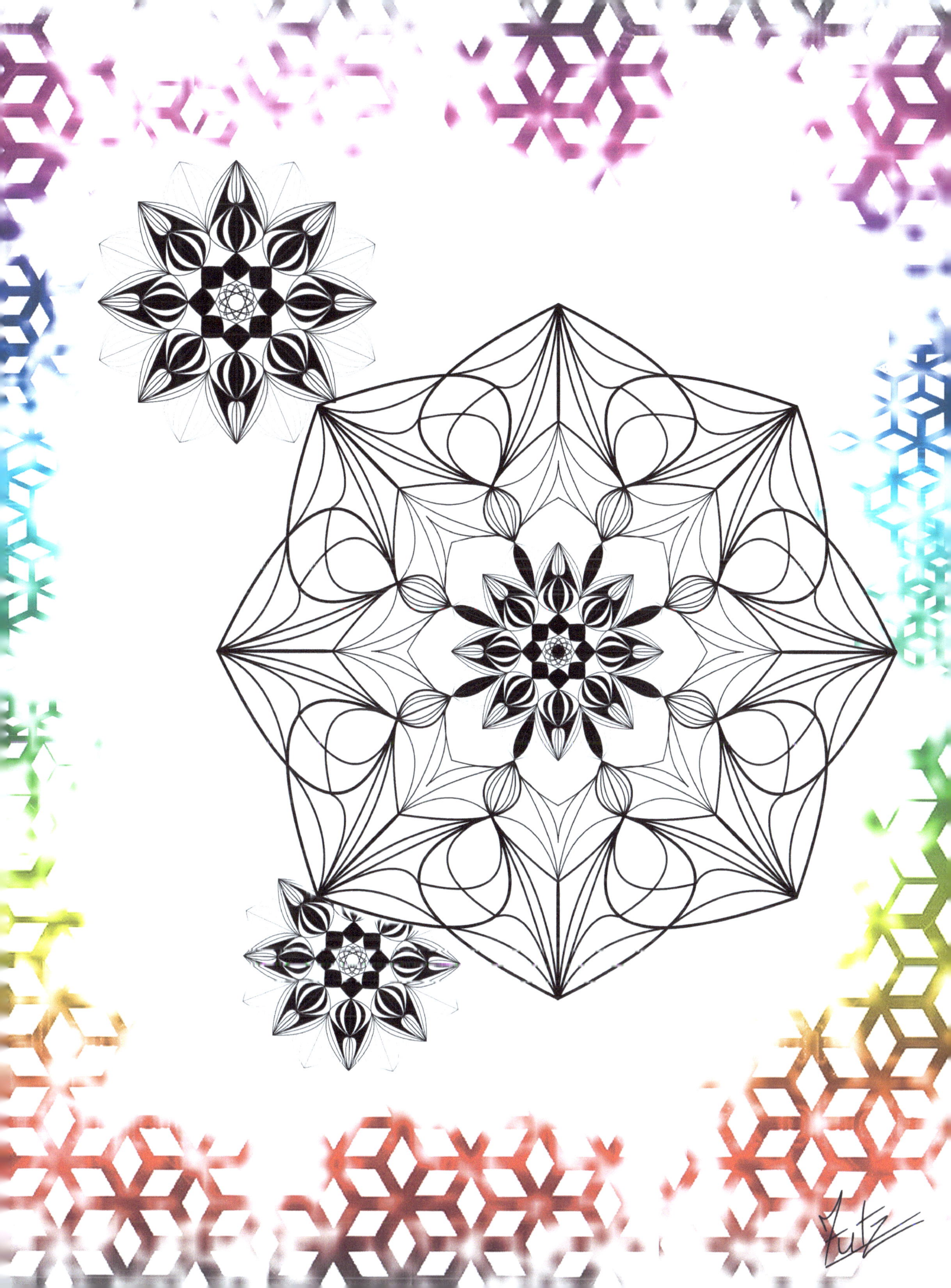

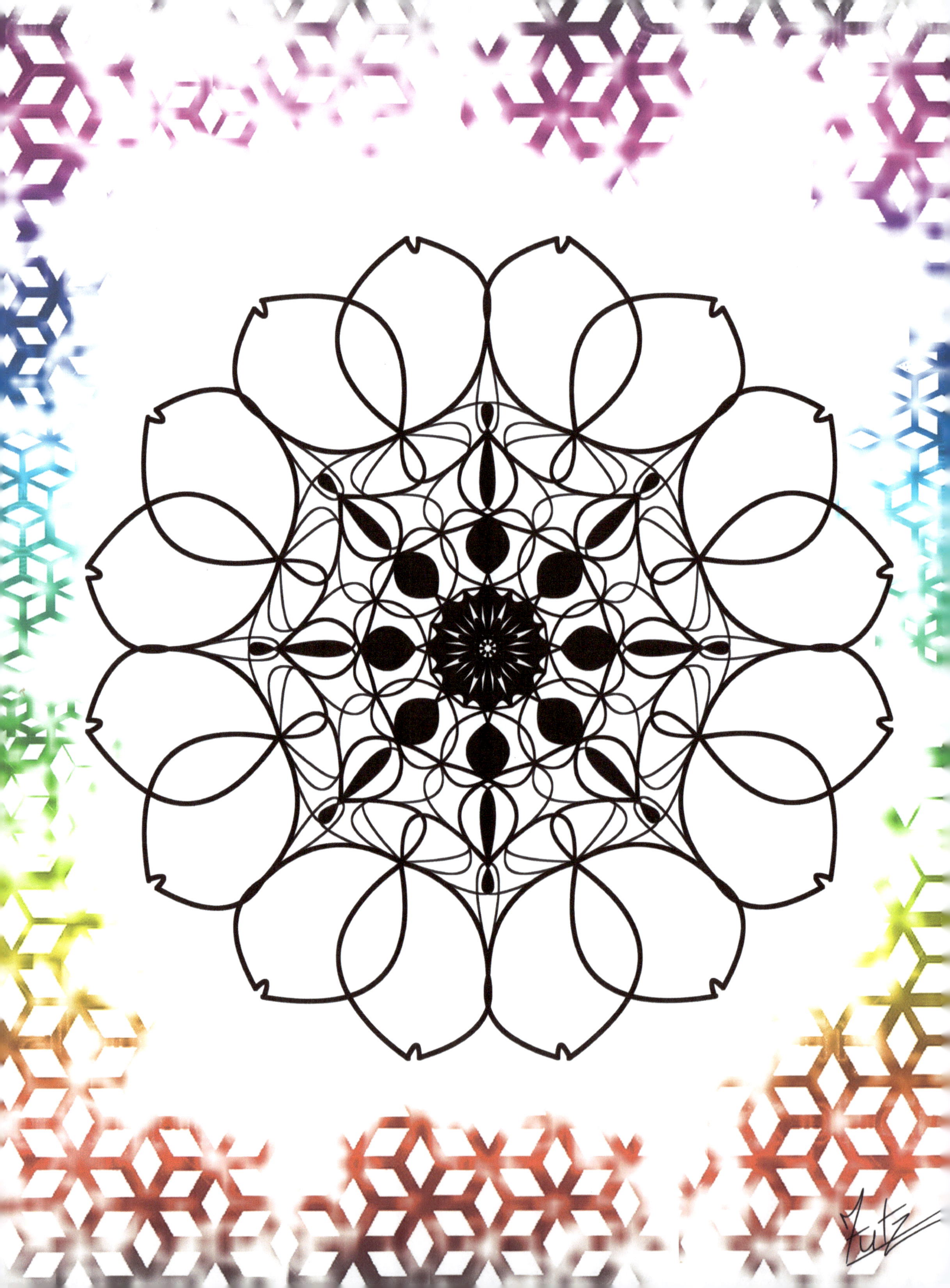

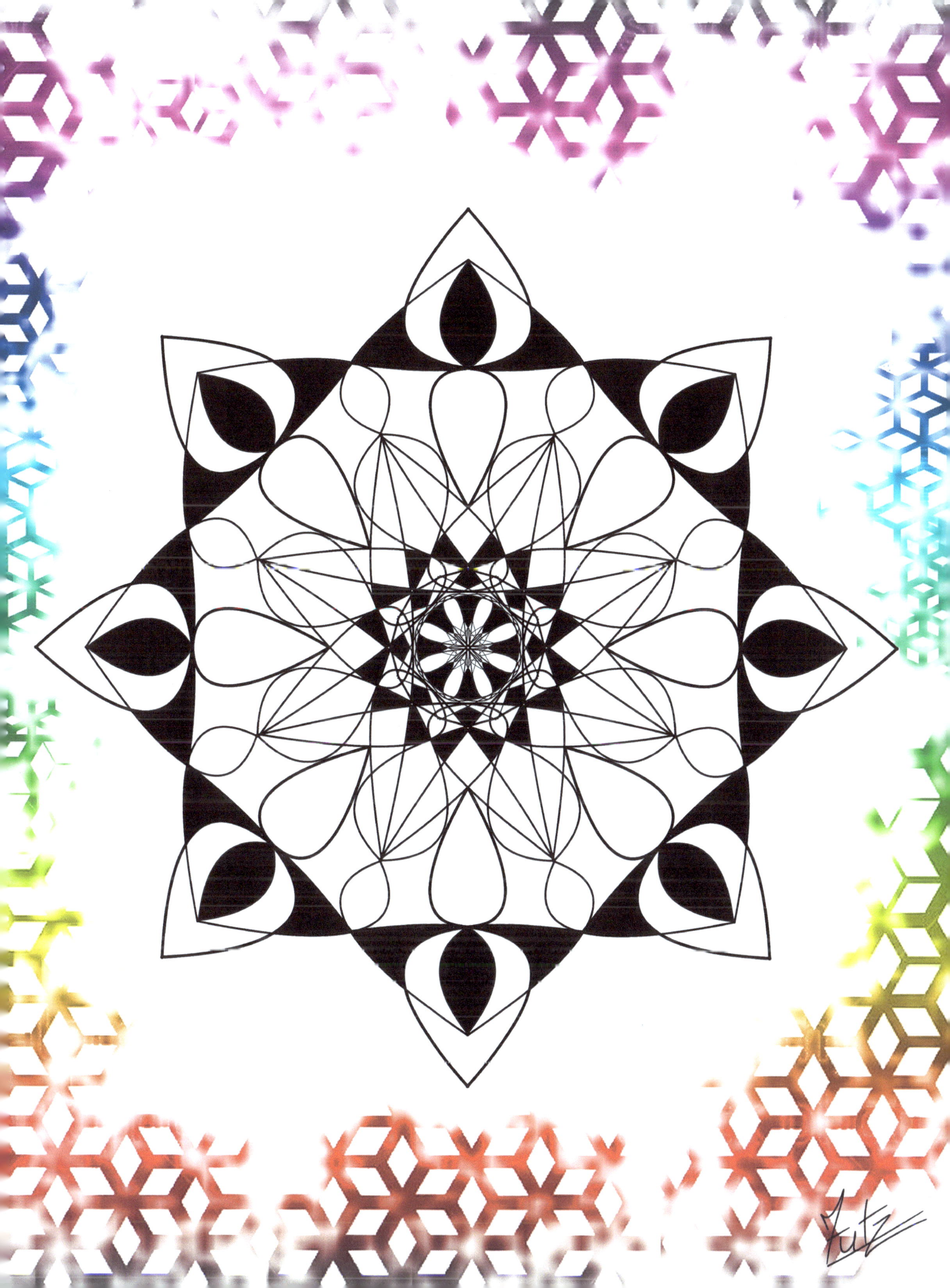

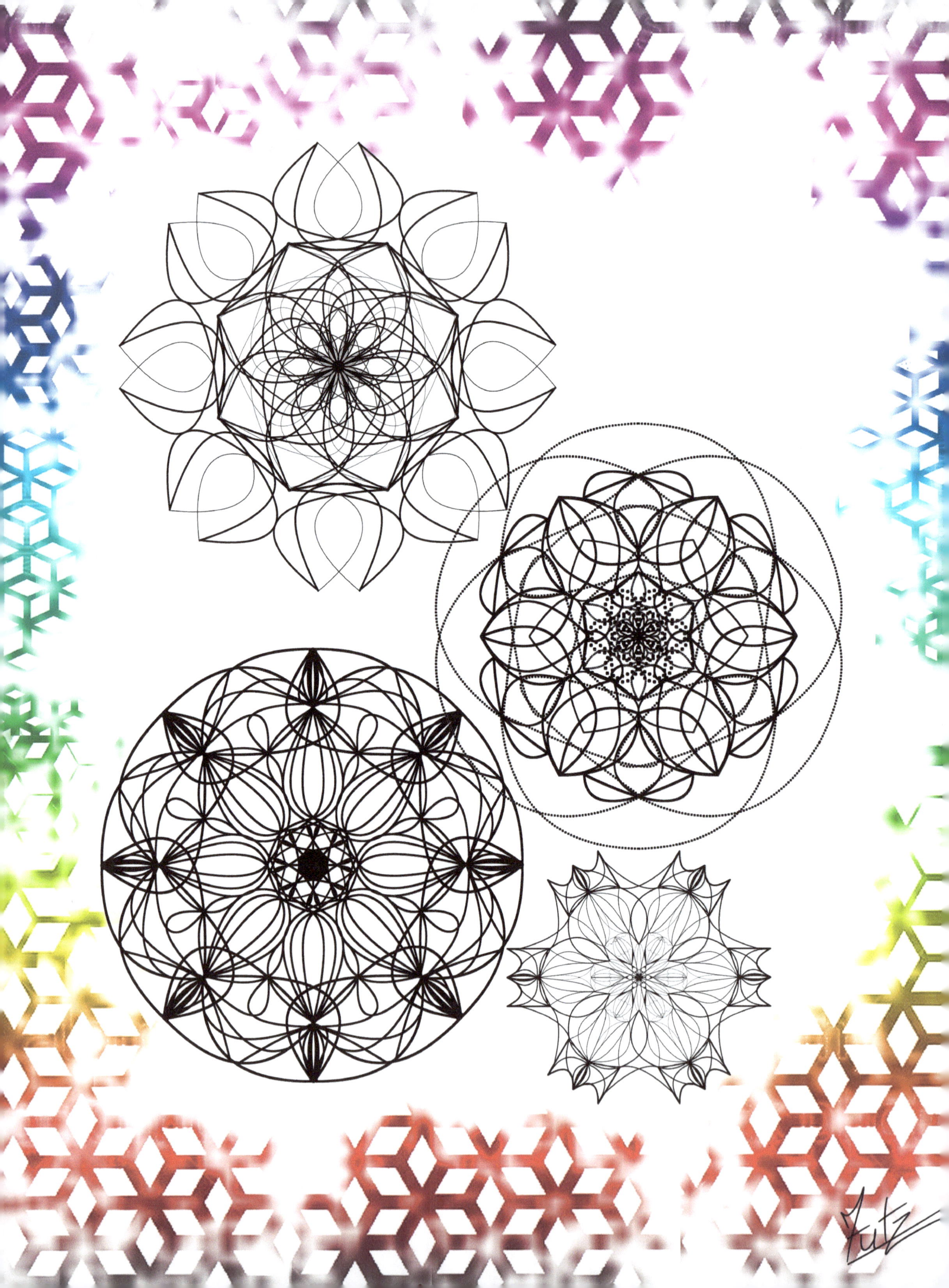

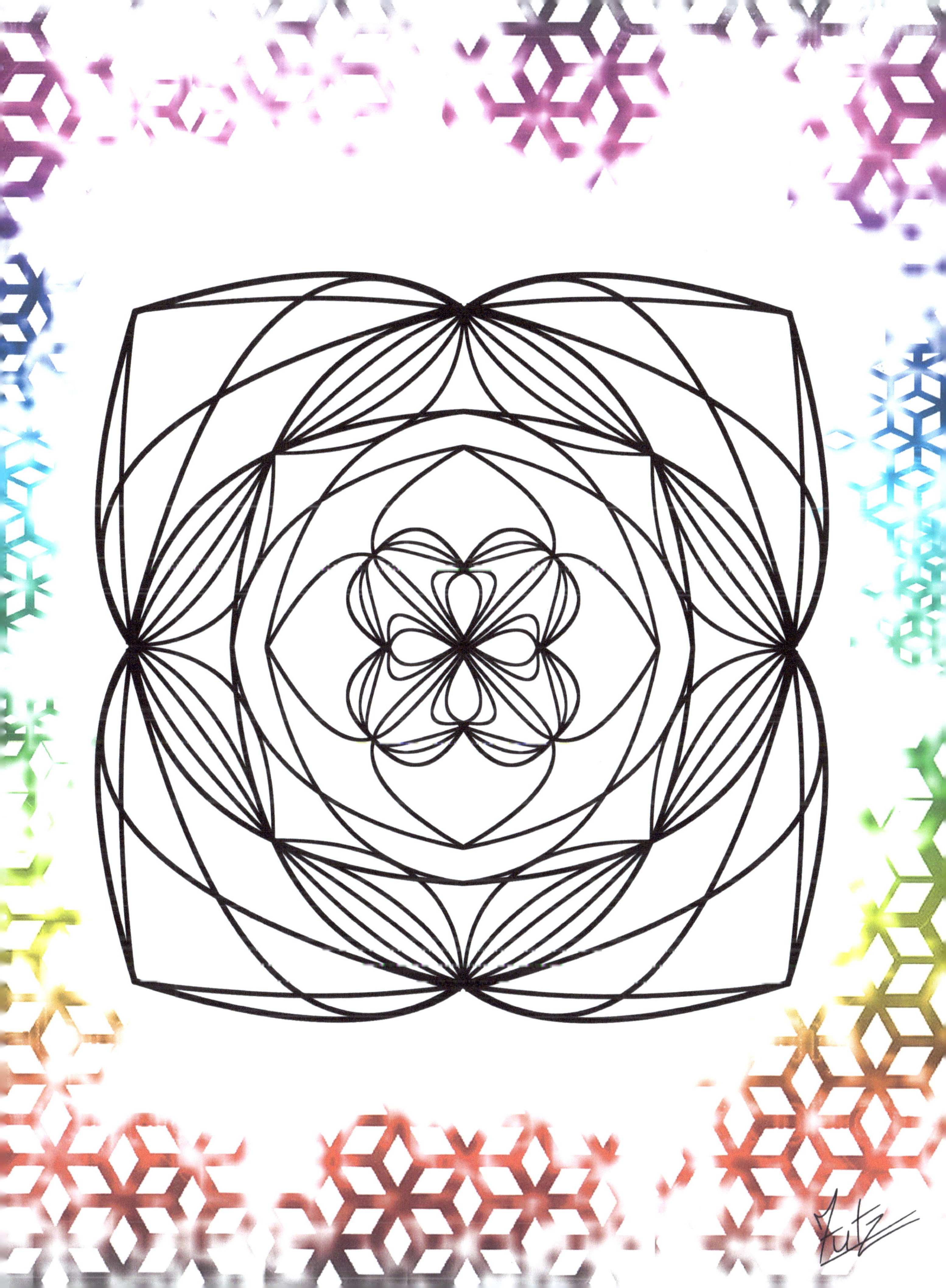
Lutz

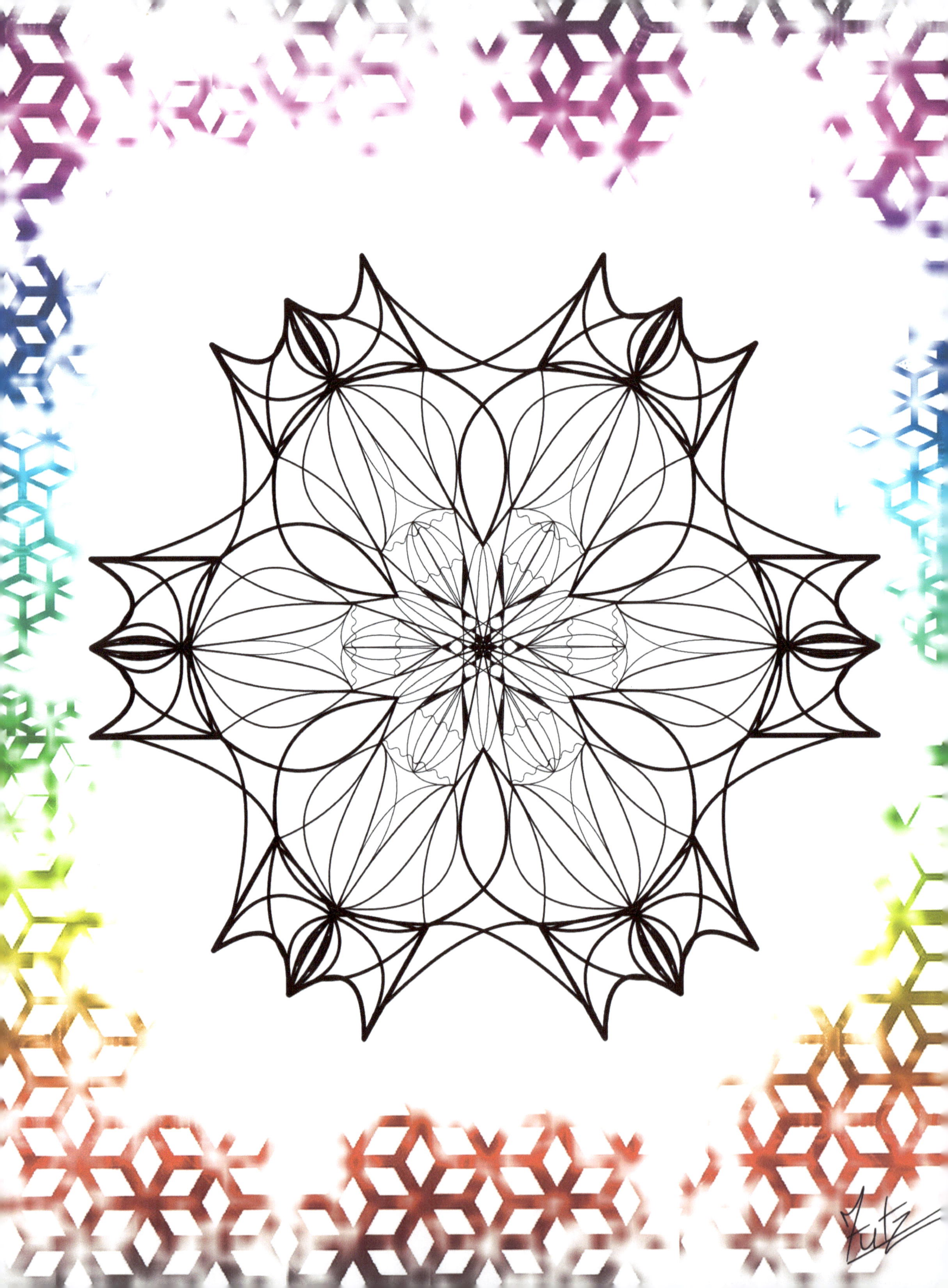

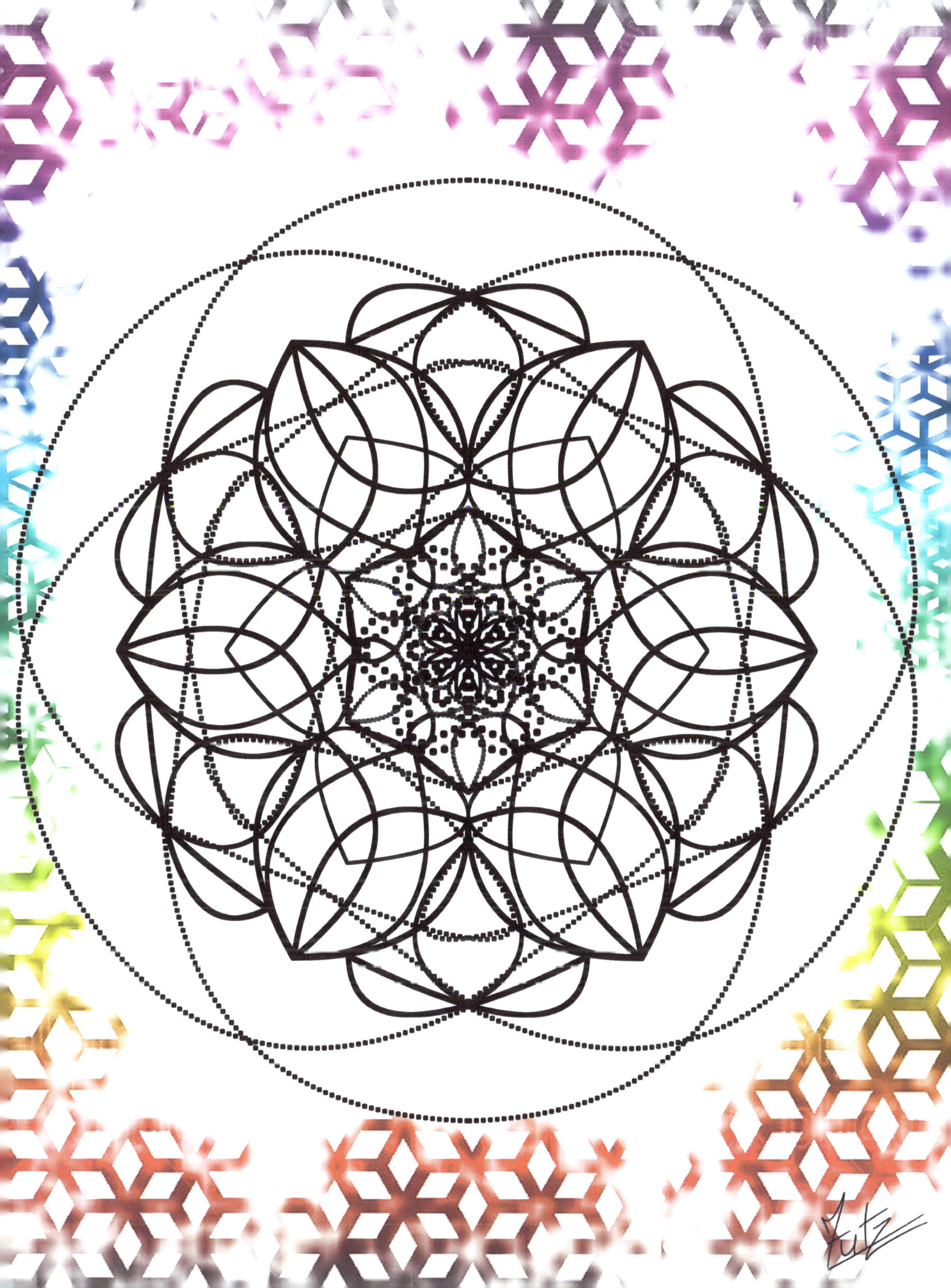

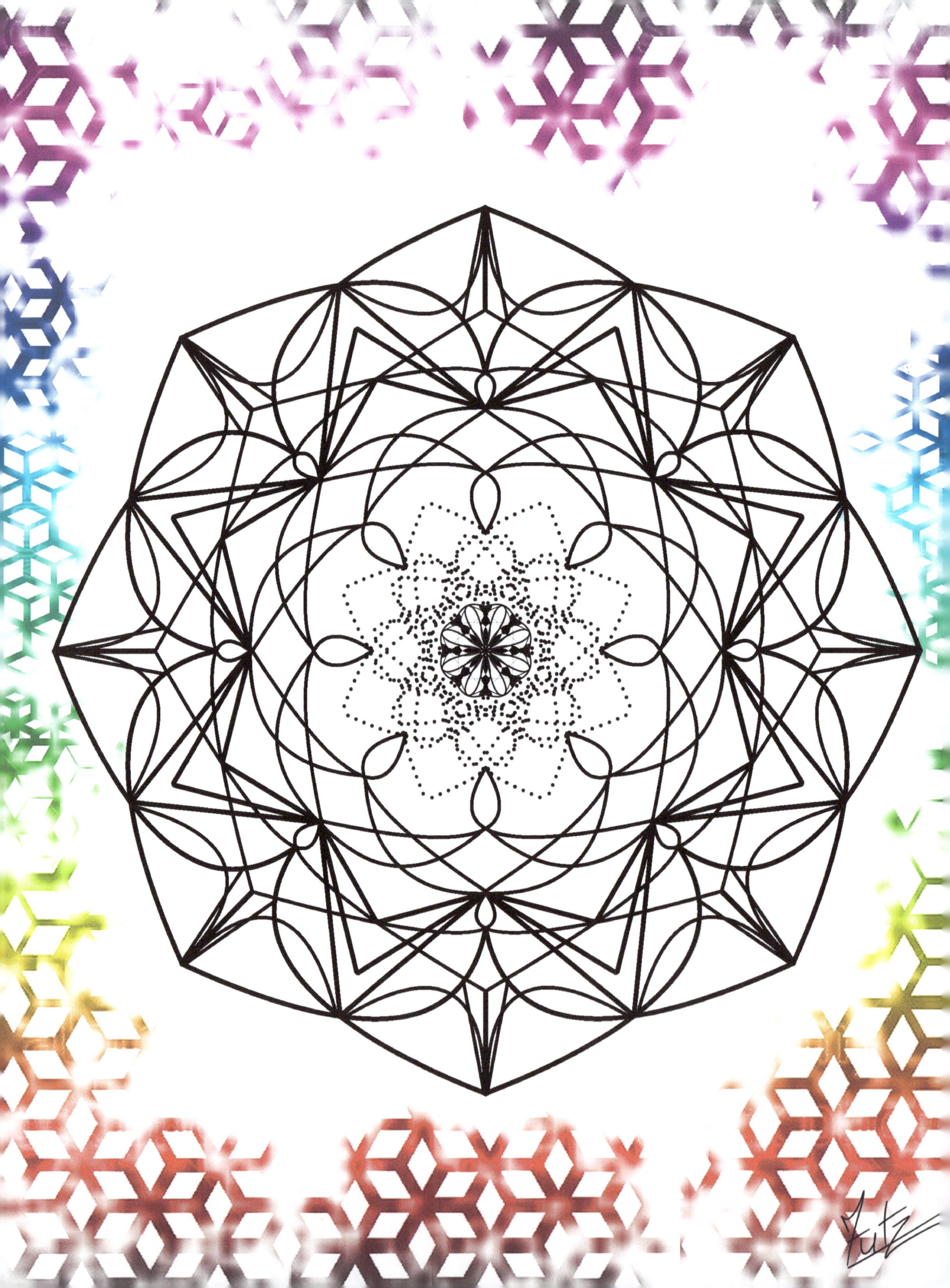

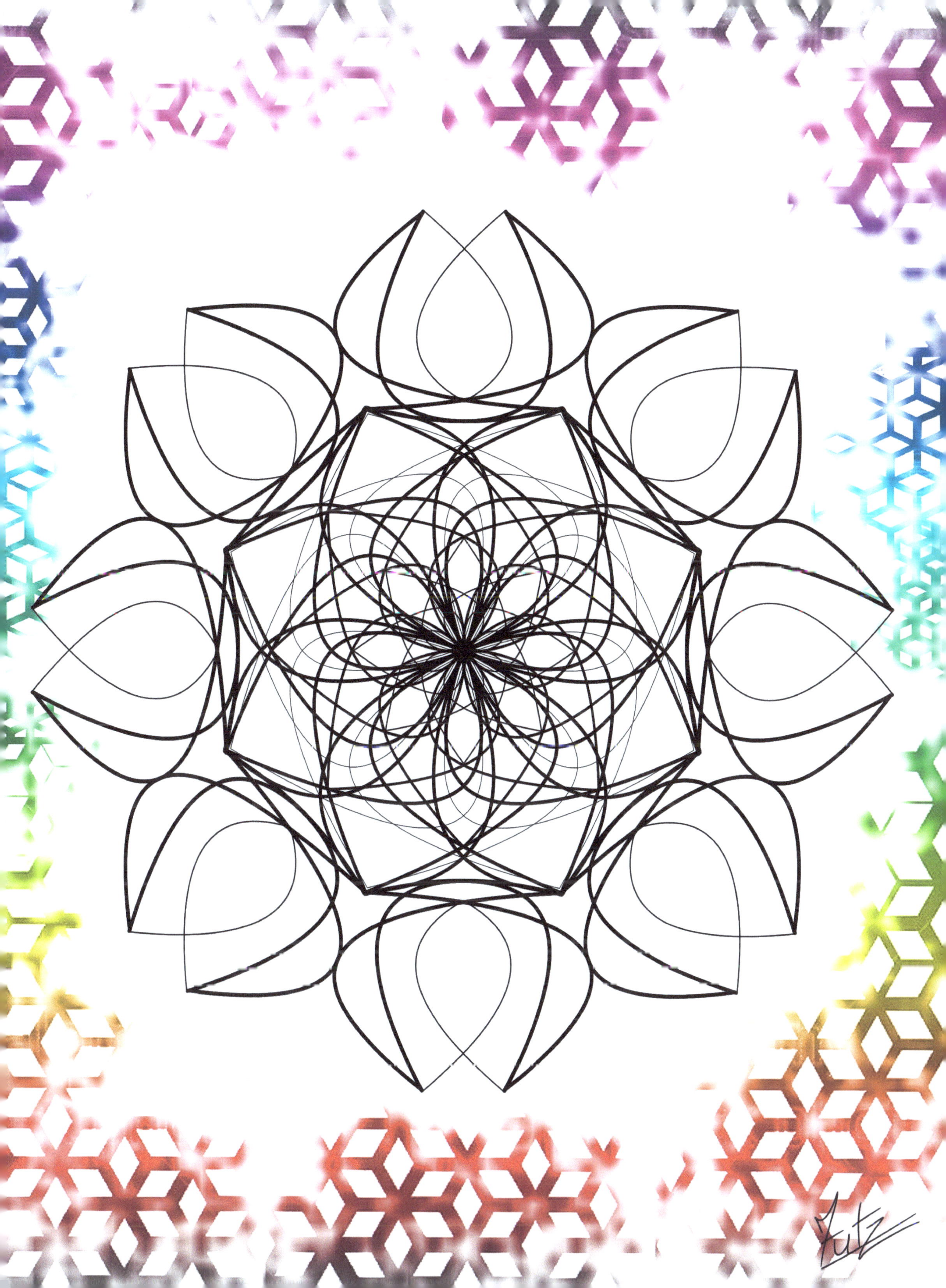

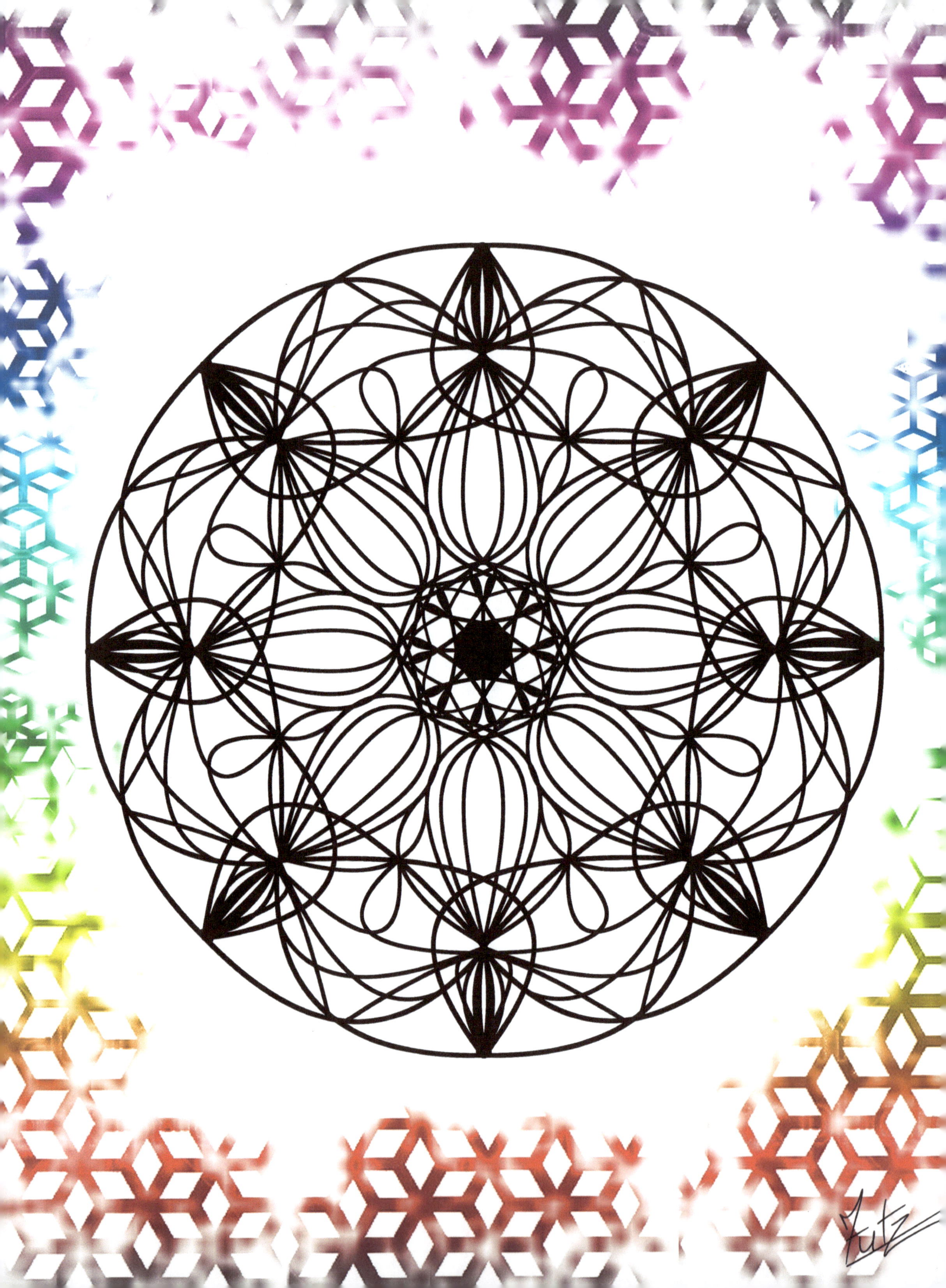

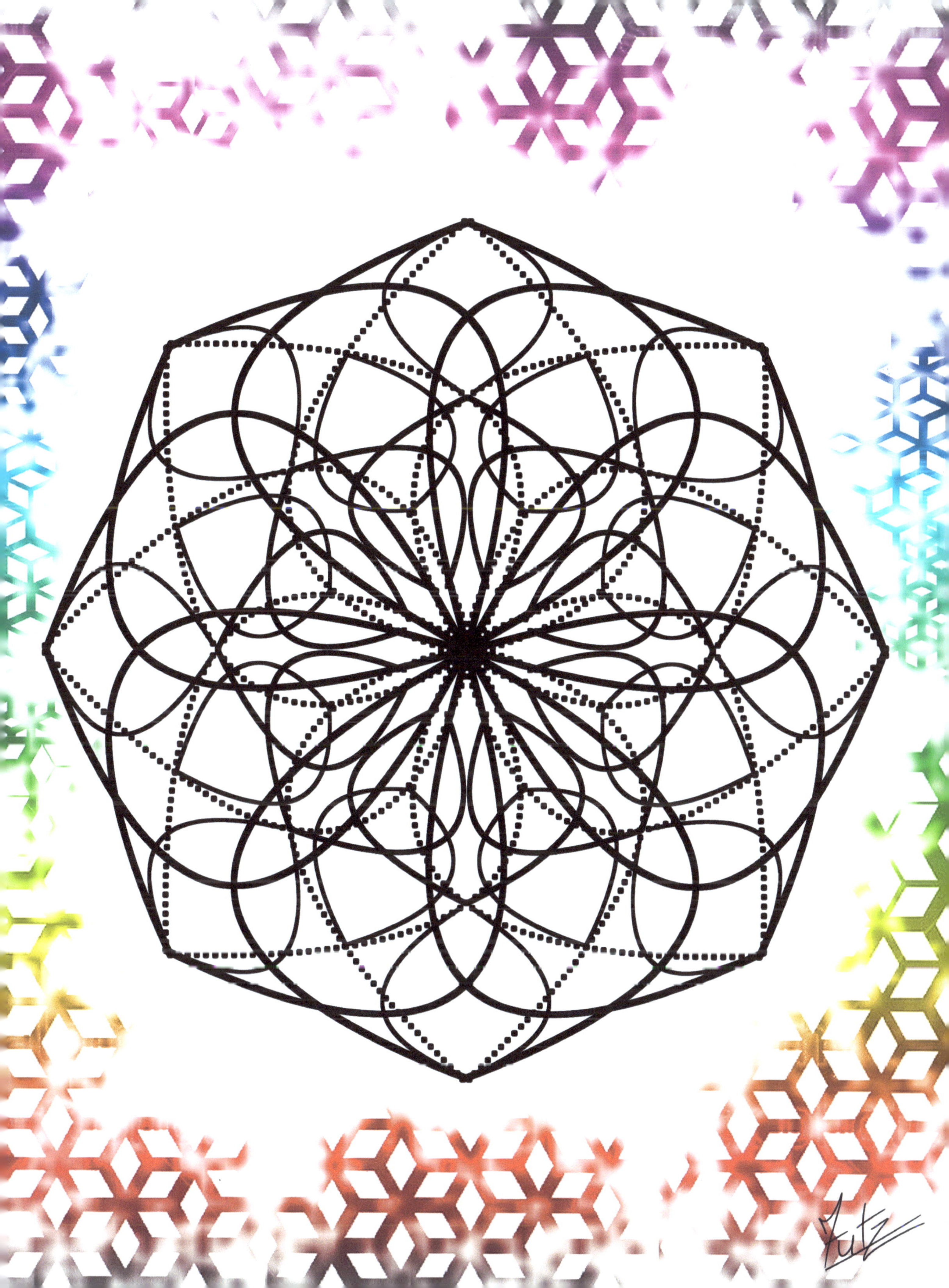

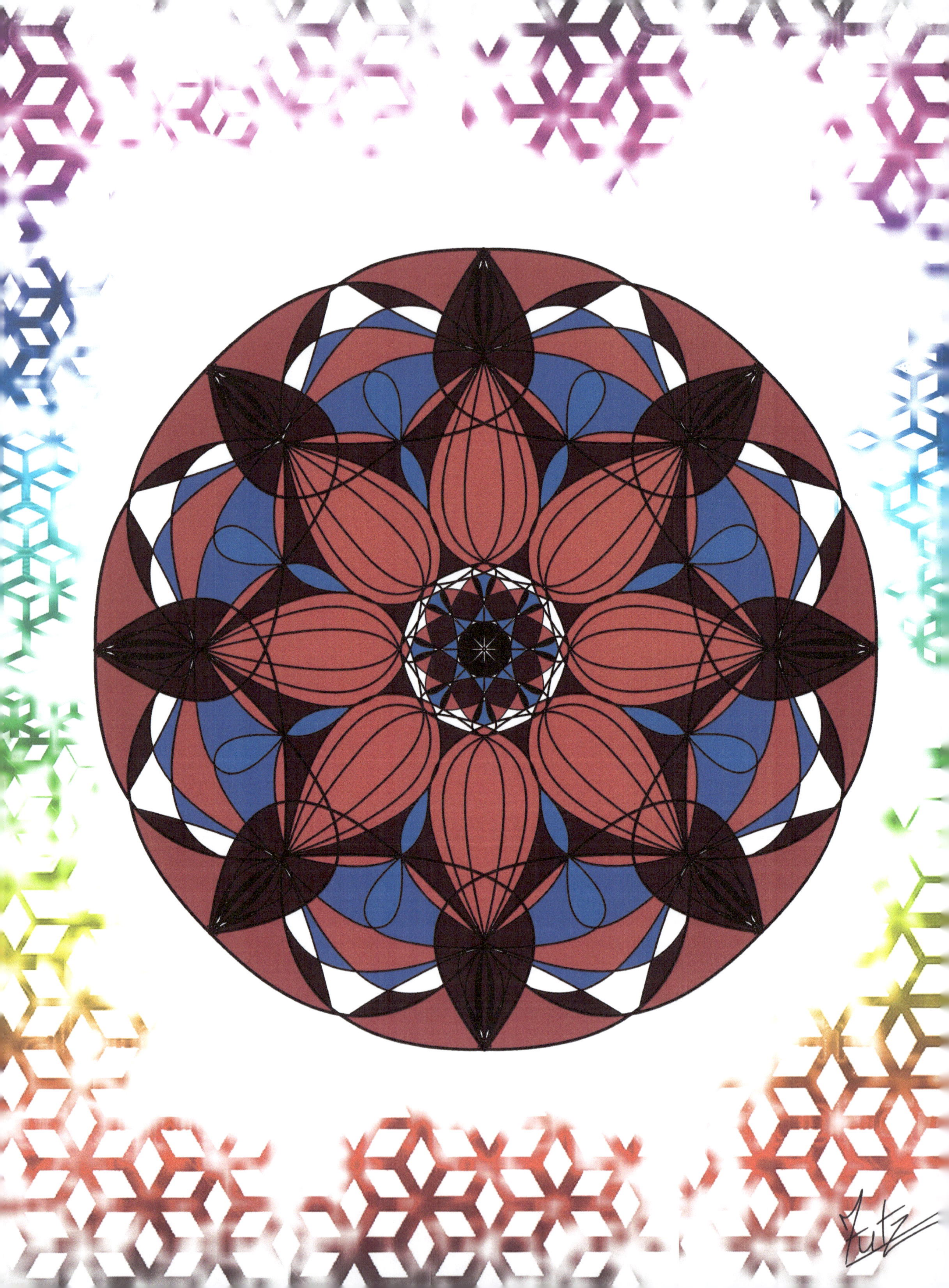

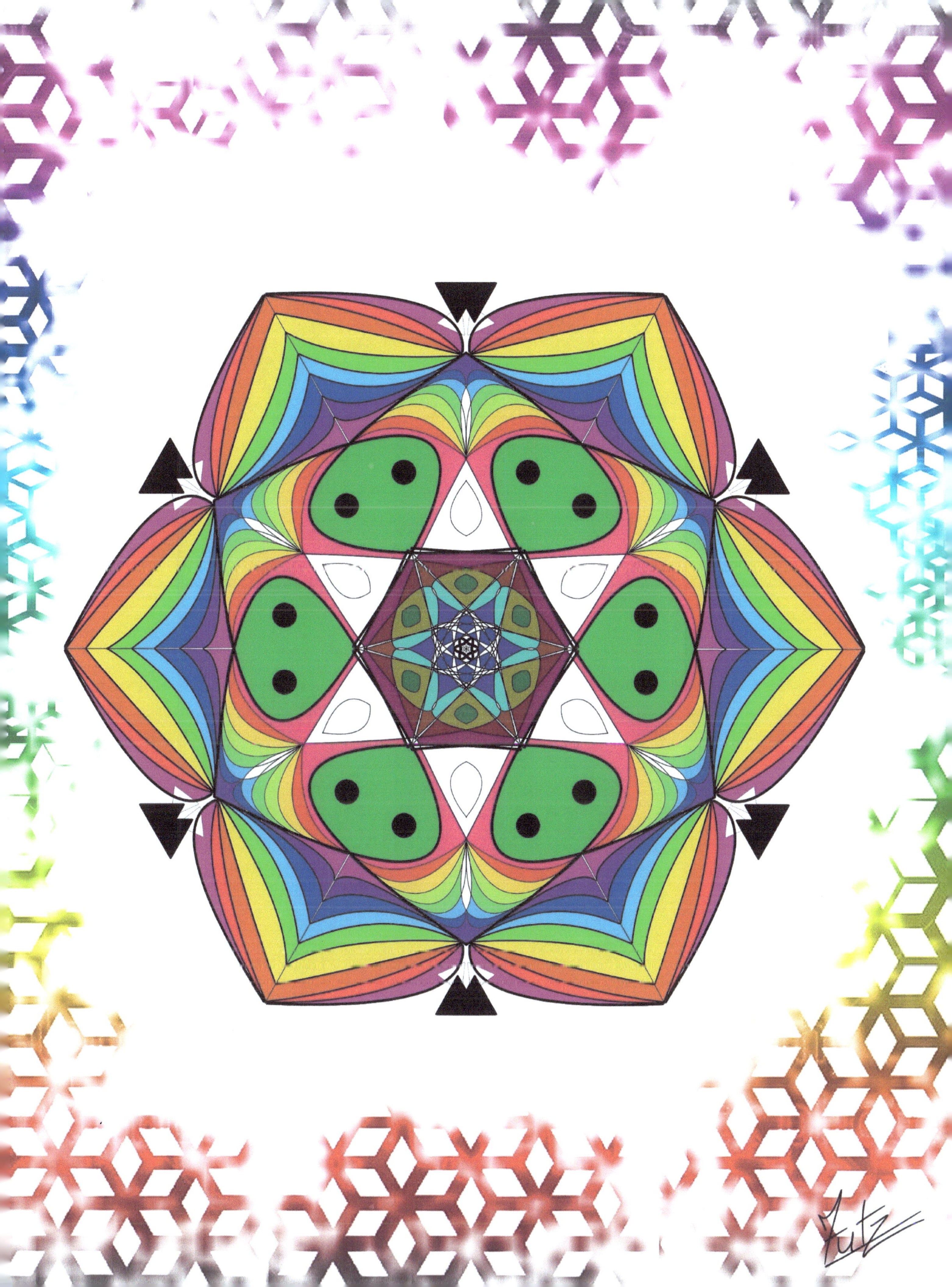

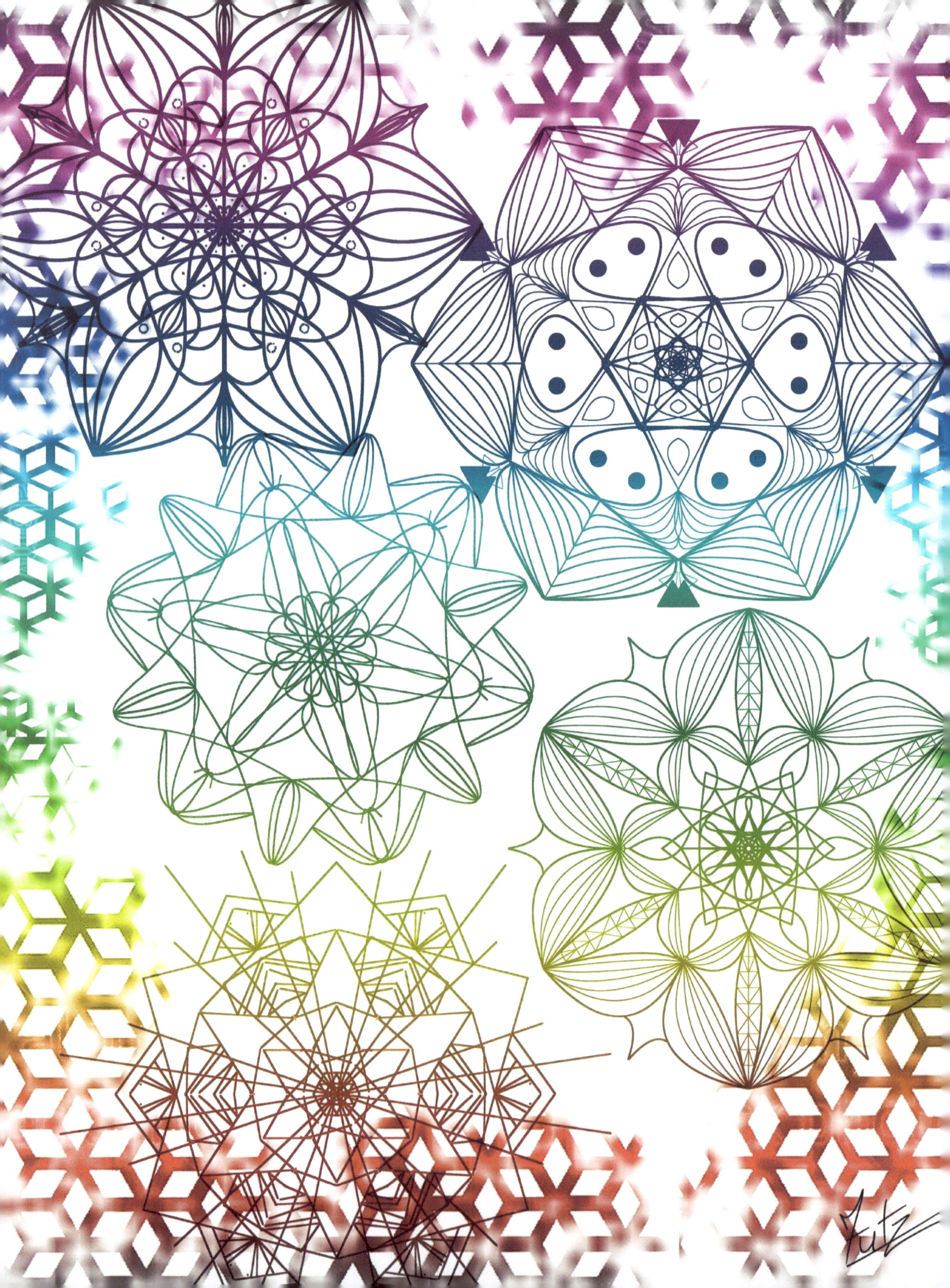